CHURCH MUSIC SOCIETY PUBLICATION: 023A
Hon. General Editor: Richard Lyne

for the Choir and Congregation of St. Mary's Church, North Leigh, Oxon.

Saint Mary's Mass

Music by ANTHONY CÆSAR

Kyrie

Unison Voices

Andante con moto

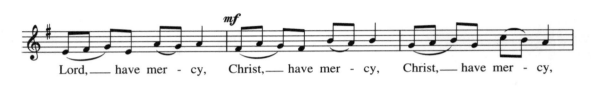

Lord, —— have mer - cy,

Lord, —— have mer - cy, Christ, —— have mer - cy, Christ, —— have mer - cy,

Lord, —— have mer - cy, Lord, —— have mer - cy, have mer - cy.

Alternative version of Kyrie

Ky - ri - e e - le - i - son,

Ky - ri - e e - le - i - son, Chris - te e - le - i - son, Chris - te e - le - i - son,

Ky - ri - e e - le - i - son, Ky - ri - e e - le - i - son.

Printed in Great Britain

Gloria

Glo - ry to God in the high - est, and peace to his peo-ple on earth. — Lord God, hea - ven-ly King, al- migh - ty God and Fa - ther, we wor - ship you, we give you thanks, we praise you for your glo - ry.

Lord — Je - sus Christ, on - ly Son of the Fa - ther, Lord God, Lamb of God, you take a - way the sin of the world: have mer - cy on us: you are seat - ed at the right hand of the Fa - ther: re - ceive our prayer.

Tempo primo

For you — a-lone are the Ho-ly One, you a-lone are the Lord,—

cresc.

you a-lone are the Most High, Je-sus Christ, with the Ho-ly Spi-rit,

allargando *ff*

in the glo-ry of God — the Fa-ther. A — men. A — men.

Gospel Responses

mf

Glo — ry to Christ — our Sa — viour.

mf *f*

Praise — to Christ — our Lord. —

Sanctus – Benedictus

Andante solenne *pp*

Ho-ly, Ho-ly, Ho-ly Lord, God — of pow'r and

più mosso *mf* *f*

might, heav'n — and earth are full — of your glo-ry. Ho-san-na in the

mf

high-est. Bless-ed is he who comes — in the name — of the

f *ff*

Lord. Ho-san-na in the high-est, Ho-san-na in the high-est.

Acclamations

Agnus Dei

Acknowledgment

The *Gloria*, the *Sanctus*, the *Benedictus* and the *Agnus Dei* from *The Order for Holy Communion Rite A* from the Alternative Service Book 1980 are © International Consultation on English Texts and are reproduced with permission of the Central Board of Finance of the Church of England.

Origination by Jeanne Fisher, Ludlow, Shropshire
Printed by Halstan & Co. Ltd., Amersham, Bucks

Pack of 10 copies
Not available separately

ISBN 0-19-395363-3